History of Korea after 1945

Korea, the divided country after World War II

Janina Hansell

Table of Contents

I. The Situation after the Second World War

At the end of the Second World War in 1945, Japan surrendered unconditionally. This had a huge impact on Korea as the country located on the Korean peninsula **became a Japanese colony in 1910**. So the question was how the victorious countries USA and Russia would deal with Korea. Even when the end of the war was foreseeable, the two great powers made a decision. **They divided Korea into North and South** and both accepted that this division would be temporary. **The dividing line ran along the 38th Parallel**. History should show that this boundary line solidified.

By 1948, a government regime was established in the North, built and controlled by the Soviet Union, while the United States helped to establish a military government in the South. **The Soviets helped Kim Il-sung (1912 – 1994)** to exercise governmental power, and **the Americans provided substantial support to Rhee Syng-man (1875 – 1965)**.

Note: In Korea the surname is preceded by the first name. Kim and Rhee are the surnames; Il-sung and Syng-man are the first names.

But the two Korean parts they ruled were neither independent nor sovereign; in fact, they were regarded as puppets of the Soviet Union or the USA. The **Cold War** determined the political atmosphere, and the two great powers watched with suspicion to ensure that no advantage could arise for the counterpart. During this period, **Harry Truman**, a member of the Democratic Party, ruled as president of the United States and **Josef Stalin** was the general secretary of the Central Committee of the Communist Party of the Soviet Union and the chairman of the Council of People's Commissars. From 1946, he was also the chairman of the Council of Ministers of the Soviet Union (USSR); in fact, he was a dictator.

The entire country of Korea was still suffering from the consequences of the Second World War, but especially from the decades of Japanese domination, which had exploited their colony economically enormously. In the North, land reforms were carried out, in which the **pri-**

vate property was converted into state property. These were the same processes and events that the Soviet Union had experienced. **Women's suffrage** was introduced in 1946.

The call for land reforms became louder and louder in the South. The Americans had little knowledge about Korean conditions. In particular, it was difficult for them to manage the country properly without knowledge of its culture and language. But they initiated fundamental reforms, which were carried out until 1950 and in which **private property was maintained as a principle**. Together with Rhee, they mainly represented the principle of preventing communism from spreading in the North. They confiscated the land belonging to the Japanese colonial rulers and distributed it. Thus, the huge estates and their owners disappeared, and many smaller estates were established as family businesses. In 1949, the government for the first time created a law that seriously affected the educational situation and introduced **compulsory education**.

The divided Korea was a novelty in the history of the country. The goal of finding a common midway leading to unification remained unachieved. The main reason for this is that neither the USA nor the Soviet Union was ready to compromise. Neither left the Korean region they supported; rather, they ensured that their candidates remained in power. The North pursued an expansion to the South and the South pursued an expansion to the North.

II. The Foundations of the State

In 1947 and 1948, the United Nations and the United States finally called for elections to be held throughout Korea. The Soviets rejected this proposal, so elections were held only in South Korea.

It was the first time in the country's four-millennia-old history that the Koreans were allowed to appoint a government. So far they had been ruled by the emperors of China, Korean dynasties and the Japanese. But this was not going to be easy. Before the elections, the Russians threatened the deprivation of electricity, which they delivered from the North to the South. The Americans reacted furiously, claiming that the Russians, as they did in Germany, would seek a puppet government, followed by a full seizure of power.

The South Koreans did not elect the communists, instead they elected democratic parties. Because of the communist attacks on the electorate in South Korea, heavily armed American forces accompanied the election. Hodge, the leading general, praised his soldiers as the midwives of a new nation. Those who could not write (and they were not few) expressed their will with an ink fingerprint.

A **National Assembly** was founded and a **constitution** was passed. Also there was a parliamentary representation of the people. This led in **August 1948 to the foundation of the Republic of Korea with a government domiciled in Seoul**. It was the birth of the 1st Republic of Korea.

In **September 1948**, the North followed suit and **founded the Democratic People's Republic of Korea with its government located in Pyongyang**. Both states claimed to be the only legitimate Korea and did not accept the other as legitimate. Neither region could be regarded as a stable state. The North and the South insisted that they wanted to integrate the other part into their own half of Korea, with the possibility that this might lead to hostilities. In fact, border disputes with violent assaults were common all the time.

The president and dictator in North Korea, as expected, was **Kim Il-sung**, who represented Stalinist communism and ruled until his death. He was the grandfather of Kim Jong-un, who was appointed "chief leader" of the Democratic People's Republic of Korea in December 2011. Kim Il-sung was also politically active in his youth and followed Marxism and therefore came into conflict with the law. Despite an arrest at young age, he later fought against the Japanese in a partisan group.

In the South, **Rhee Syng-man** became president, and he remained until his resignation in 1960. He was descended from nobility but his family no longer held any possessions. He also came into conflict with the law because as a student he participated in anti-monarchist protest movements. As a result of this, he was imprisoned for six years. During this time he entered the Christian Methodist church. Afterwards he spent some time in the USA, where he completed his doctorate. Back in Korea, he fought against the Japanese, so he had to leave the country temporarily. **In the same way as Kim Il-sung represented Stalinism, the most violent form of communism, Rhee Syng-**

man was a vehement anti-communist. Both statesmen were at that time in charge of the government. The two great powers withdrew as far as possible from the decision-making processes of the governments and from influencing them.

III. The Korean War (1950 – 1953)

1. Invasion

After repeated clashes at the border, the North Korean army marched into South Korea on **25 June 1950**, deliberately and clearly crossing the border. The attack was well planned. Thanks to the Soviet Union's help in building up the state apparatus, North Korea had an operational, powerful army of more than 130,000 soldiers with artillery, while the South could only show around 100,000 soldiers ad hoc. The US had no intention of equipping it with comparable military means because they wanted to avoid an invasion of the North. But now the USA prepared itself militarily for a war against the communist troops.

2. First Stage

The first stage was to push the communists out of South Korea. But the American soldiers were not up to the climatic conditions. In the extremely hot summer, they drank water from rice fields and contracted serious diseases. Even the Korean army could not withstand the well-trained opponent. A retreat was necessary.

The United States intervened with the **United Nations Security Council**. The result was that several Western nations declared their solidarity with South Korea. First and foremost, Great Britain, Canada and Australia sent auxiliary troops. But before they arrived, the North Koreans had to be resisted on their own territory. The general responsible, **General Walton Walker**, gave a famous speech in front of the American soldiers from which the words "**stand or die**" go down in history. He made it clear that there must be no further retreat. In fact, the weak troops held back their opponents for weeks but with immense losses.

3. Second Stage

In the second stage, **General Douglas MacArthur** turned the tables upside down with help of the armed forces, which were now an army of the United Nations. He was the successor of Walker, who had died in a car accident. MacArthur dared a risky attack on the northwestern port city of **Incheon**, which was an economically and strategically important point. It was occupied by the North Koreans. He managed to recapture it and, thus, standing behind the enemy lines, prevented the supply and communication possibilities of the North Korean army. A simultaneous attack on the enemy troops in Seoul led to panic among the North Koreans and the capital was recaptured. This was the situation in September 1950, but then the Chinese entered the game.

4. Third Stage

In the third stage of the war, China sent troops to support North Korea. The huge empire was keen to preserve **North Korea as a buffer state**. The American president Truman had originally the goal to bring Korea to a reunification and to let it be governed according to the West. Therefore, MacArthur and his troops crossed the border of the 38th parallel. He even advanced to the Yalu, the border river of North Korea and China. But here the Chinese attacked him with about 180,000 men. MacArthur had to retreat.

President Truman saw the conflict with the Chinese as a great danger, especially since the communist leader of China, Mao Tse-tung, clearly threatened a serious war if the Americans did not stay away from the Yalu border.

Therefore, Truman now signaled his readiness for a ceasefire in the Korean War. MacArthur, however, did everything he could to continue provoking China because he wanted the war with the communists and a final victory over them. He was dismissed from military service by Truman in April 1951 for refusing to obey the contrary order. Peace talks began in July of the same year.

5. Fourth Stage

In the fourth stage, the peace negotiations dragged on until mid-1953, when no agreement could be reached on where the border was to run and where the prisoners of war were to remain. During this time, there were repeated battles at the 38th parallel, which were not even forbidden in the negotiations.

6. The Armistice

Then a historically significant event occurred. President Truman's period as a president was over; he was no longer a candidate. His successor was **the Republican David Eisenhower** on 20 January 1953. A second event, which was no less important, followed on 5 March of the same year. Stalin died and **Nikita Khrushchev** became his successor. He initiated the de-Stalinisation of the Soviet Union. This also created new conditions for the Korean War.

Eisenhower was exerting pressure to bring peace negotiations to an end. He threatened his communist opponents with the use of nuclear weapons, and South Korea, for its part, was to yield to some demands.

As a result, on 27 July 1953, a **ceasefire** was negotiated by the United Nations and North Korea. The outline of the border was determined near the 38th degree of latitude (the current status of the troops was considered decisive, South Korea thus gained approx. 1500 square kilometers). Along the border the **demilitarised zone**, **DMZ**, was created. Representatives of neutral countries decided on the fate of the prisoners of war. They agreed that each prisoner should decide for himself whether to stay where he was or return to his homeland.

These arrangements should apply until a "final peaceful solution" was found. But there was no peace treaty.

7. Summary

About five million people died in the Korean War. The civilians who died accounted for about 10% of the deaths in the war. The last consequence was a war of **West against East, the**

free world against communism. The Americans were frustrated because it was quite new for them not to be able to force capitulation. Many American citizens, like General MacArthur, could not understand why the United States had not forced a war with China. But it is thanks to the prudence of the government that this was not the case. A third world war could easily have resulted.

IV. The Further Development of the 1st Republic of South Korea

The south of the peninsula remained under the influence of America after the Korean War. President Rhee wanted to continue his invasion of North Korea in order to reunite Korea under Western-oriented leadership. But it did not meet with Eisenhower's approval. However, the US supported the South Korean country's economic and political development and also helped in rebuilding the military. Nevertheless, there was **mismanagement and corruption**. In the second half of the decade, riots therefore repeatedly occurred, culminating in a **massive student protest in 1960**, after the March elections. Rhee's Liberal Party wins with almost 90%. The reason for this was **electoral fraud**.

The day before the election, Democratic Party supporters demonstrated and were shot at by police officers; eight people were killed, including students. On April 18, the students of Seoul University demanded new elections. Right-wing youth organisations, spurred on by the government attacking the students in their protests, and several other universities and students joined forces. **On April 19, about 30,000 students formed a demonstration in Seoul.** They called for "New elections!" and "Democracy!" and demanded the resignation of the Rhee government. Despite the shelling with tear gas, they moved on to the Blue House, the location of the president. At the end of this day 130 people had died and more than 1000 were injured. Rhee declared **martial law** and imposed a **curfew**.

A few days later, the president made concessions, in which he went as far as to offer to break off all the ties with the Liberal Party. But the protests were still growing, and professors were also joining them. They also demanded **Rhee's resignation**. At further rallies there were more deaths. Finally, a general refused to shoot at the demonstrators and also opposed the Rhee government.

The Americans started to intervene. They demanded "**the holding of re-elections and the guarantee of freedom of expression and assembly.**" Under pressure from the USA, Rhee resigned in April and was taken to Hawaii by the CIA. And there were new elections.

V. The 2nd Republic of South Korea (1960 – 1961)

The Democratic Party won the new elections in July 1960. **Yun Bo-seon** became the president. However, the 2nd Republic was only granted a term of eight months. During this time there were about 2000 demonstrations. The strong regimentation from the Rhee era was lifted and individual freedoms were allowed. People were also allowed to form organisations. As a result, unions were formed, e.g. for journalists and for teachers. Many student groups continued to be active and succeeded in removing anti-democratic forces from the military and police apparatus. The presidency had practically only representative significance. The National Assembly determined the policy.

But the republic remained economically unstable. The currency (from 1953 to 1962 the Hwan, then the Won) lost fifty percent of its value (compared to the dollar) from 1960 to 1961. At the same time, prices rose and unemployment increased. The government could not achieve the promised positive developments, especially in the economic supply of the population.

In this situation, **Park Chung-hee (1917 – 1979)**, supported by like-minded people in a well-organised but small group, ventured **a military coup on 16 May 1961**. He came from a peasant background. Until the end of the Second World War he was a member of the military in the empire. Afterwards he joined the police in South Korea. Because he participated in a police uprising against the Rhee regime, he was arrested and sentenced to death. He escaped execution because he named other participants who were considered communist-friendly. They did not escape the death penalty. Rhee himself remained with the police, from whom parts of the army were later recruited.

He was a general at the time of the coup. Under his rule, a two-year transitional period followed, during which the military exerted strong influence on South Korean politics. It was practically a **military government**. During this time, Park secured his political future by eliminating his opponents. Several thousand politicians lost their positions.

VI. The 3rd Republic of South Korea (1961 – 1971)

For two years Park led the republic with the help of the military. In 1963, he proclaimed the 3rd Republic and held presidential elections, which were essentially correct. Park won with 46% of the votes. In 1967, he was even re-elected with 52%. The military government was replaced; there was again a National Assembly and political freedoms.

Nevertheless, Park emphasised anti-communism so strongly that opposition politicians very easily suspected that they were pro-communists and thus sympathisers with North Korea. He created an **economic development agency** and the **Korean Central Intelligence Service KCIA**. Both supported him in his plans but at the same time effectively restricted the democratic rights of the National Assembly because they centrally managed decision-making processes. The Department of Economic Affairs appointed Park under the leadership of the deputy prime minister with high-ranking scientists.

On one hand, Park wanted to promote strong economic development of the country, which is why at the beginning of the 3rd Republic he initiated a five-year plan. On the other hand, he did not integrate his measures into democratic processes. For him, economic progress was more important than anything else. That is why his measures were often referred to as "**development dictatorship**". Reunification with North Korea was not one of his primary goals. Rather, he followed the motto: first the development of South Korea, and later the reunification. His goals were, as he stated in a program:

- Strengthening nationalism

- Fighting communism

- Making people responsible for themselves

- Presenting the Republic of Korea to the world as an internally cohesive country

He promoted education because he wanted to teach the contents of his concept to young people and he facilitated access to school education for the lower strata. At universities, he increasingly encouraged competitive thinking—also in order to counteract the political activities of budding academics and prevent domestic unrest from arising in the first place because the first loud criticisms of the regime always came from intellectual circles.

In the 1960s, Park succeeded in decisively advancing **economic development** so that by the end of the decade South Korea had **overtaken the North**. He promoted industrialisation, including the chemical industry. The workforce as well as the farming population paid low wages for the immense economic growth, although the average prosperity was rising. This was why Park launched an **initiative in 1971 to equalise the income gap**. This granted and proved success over the next few years.

The necessary capital came from abroad. The president agreed favourable conditions with Japanese and American companies in order to advance the production process and foreign trade. For example, companies that exported heavily received very cheap loans. Among other things, Park laid the foundations for the POSCO steelworks, which today ranks among the TOP FIVE steel producers.

Park succeeded in normalising relations with Japan and in 1965 adopted the **Korea-Japan Treaty** (known as the "Basic Treaty"), which provided for high reparations for the period between 1910 and 1945. However, the population missed an official apology for Japan's suffering during this period. The fact that Japan "only" financially compensated did not work out well for the population.

During his reign, Park ensured that South Korea, as the Republic of Korea is now mostly known, received greater attention on the international stage, which he achieved above all through his close relations with the USA. He supported America in the Vietnam War with about 300,000 soldiers.

VII. The 4th Republic of South Korea (1972 – 1979)

In 1971, elections were on the agenda again because constitutionally the term of the presidential office, which was endowed with much power, lasted eight years. Park had the majority in the National Assembly with his newly founded Democratic Republican Party. But he only just won the elections. His opponent, **Kim Dae-jung**, won 45% of the votes.

Kim Dae-jung was also considered a dissident and went into exile in Japan, where he worked on a political counter-movement to Park. The South Korean KCIA kidnapped him, but the American CIA rescued him—probably from his assassination by the intelligence service of his homeland. Park had him returned to South Korea, arrested and later placed under house arrest.

Park made a new constitution. A little later, it became apparent that it was rejected by over 90% of the population. Initially, he declared a **national state of emergency**. The background for this was that he feared massive political resistance due to his narrow election victory. Then he drafted the "**Yusin-Constitution**", which meant renewal, rejuvenation, modernisation and restoration. It was approved by the National Assembly in October 1972, which created the 4th Republic. It brought decisive **changes to the legal system**.

According to the new laws, the president would be re-elected for a term of six years, without limitation of the electoral periods. This would allow Park himself a third period of reign. The president could appoint 33% of the members of the National Assembly directly, thus securing a majority. The people only voted indirectly, and members of the new "National Reunification Conference", who were loyal to the regime and directly elected the president, were standing for election. Park could also issue decrees on his own. He might also control both the legislature and the judiciary. The activity of trade unions was severely restricted. In terms of educational policy, he exerted great influence on the content of textbooks. **In fact, he became a dictator**. His election in 1972 and re-election in 1978 became a mere formality.

In 1979, there were mass demonstrations against the government. **General Kim Jae-kyu** met with Park for dinner. He shot him. He justified the act with his deep conviction that only without Park would his country have a chance to return to democratic development. At that time Kim Jae-Kyu was the leader of the intelligence service, which Park himself founded.

During his reign, Park consistently pursued his line of economic development, with which he was also successful. The five-year plan paid off, a focus was placed on the expansion of heavy industry and this continued to develop. Although many loans had to be repaid abroad, there was a clear economic upswing.

In terms of foreign policy, Park began talks with North Korea and even envisaged reunification. He initiated several diplomatic relations with Western countries, including Canada. The background to this was largely that there had been rapprochement between America and China. South Korea could no longer rely on unconditional American support against the communist world and wanted to counteract isolation.

Domestically, Park found himself confronted with resistance to his undemocratic and centralist policies. In the mid-1970s, he issued emergency decrees allowing the arrest of opponents of the regime and fought vehemently against the political opposition. Nevertheless, the rebellious reactions continued, coming not only from intellectuals but also from political opponents, workers and peasants, and were radically suppressed by Park.

VIII. The Chaebol

Park had succeeded in helping South Korea to achieve enormous economic growth within a relatively short period of time, which soon eclipsed the economic conditions in the North. He achieved this through intensive **cooperation with Western companies**. However, the business was done in **close cooperation with the government**. On one hand there were interdependencies between company owners and members of the National Assembly and on the other hand family businesses with strong capital. It came to be known as the so-called chaebol.

A **chaebol** was a large company that was run by a single owner or had developed as a family business. It might have several subsidiaries, but these were centrally controlled by the owner. These might be different divisions. In reality, a chaebol was a conglomerate, but it unfolded the power of a single group because it was created and maintained by family relationships. So the management of the company was centralised and not hierarchically controlled. The interdependencies as well as the capital shares remained within the family structure and thus ensured ideal and economic cohesion. The presence on the stock market was hardly sought.

Since a chaebol was hardly subject to extensive legislation within the company, it could act much faster and adapt better to market developments than typical corporate systems. There were further advantages from the traditional links to politics. This specific corporate constellation in South Korea emerged after the country was liberated from Japanese colonial rule and was strongly driven by Park.

The South Korean chaebols became the decisive factor that made the country an international trading partner. Around the turn of the millennium, South Korea sought to make its economy more independent of family structures. But its great importance remained intact. Powerful chaebols include Hyundai Motor Group and Samsung.

IX. The Situation from 1979 to 1981

After Park's assassination, Prime Minister **Choi Kyu-hah** took over the reins of government and was president for a short time. But **General Chun Doo-hwan** risked a coup d'état and, with the help of the military, pushed him out of office. He took over the **presidency** himself after the coup in December 1979. The uprisings and demonstrations against the government were intensified. Chun, like his predecessor, applied martial law against these social unrests, most of which were carried out by students, and even tightened up the measures. In fact, there was **military rule**.

On 17 May 1980, the political situation escalated. Chun closed entire universities on the basis of the expanded martial law and curtailed press law. He arrested the leaders of a counter-movement to his regime, including the later presidents **Kim Dae-jung and Kim Young-sam**. One day later, he sent armed forces to the city of **Gwangju**, where there had been consi derable student protests. Chun had the uprising bloodily suppressed using military force.

This measure led to an increased rebellion among the students, which was also joined by many people from the population, especially those in employment. The city was in a state of revolt against the regime that fought with South Korean and American troops against the rebels. The insurgents defended them against the armed forces for nine days. The main demands were the **release of Kim Dae-jung**, the former rival candidate of Park, from prison (Kim Young-sam was not imprisoned but placed under house arrest) and the **withdrawal of martial law**.

The suppression of the revolt went down in history under the term "**massacre of Gwangju**". Eyewitnesses reported an extremely brutal action by the military, which indiscriminately used sticks and bayonets against all the people who gathered, including women, children and the elderly. Some students had to undress and were then publicly beaten. There were many deaths and injuries. The estimated number ranged between 500 and 2000.

On 27 May, the military had established peace. This was followed by numerous reprisals against critics of the regime and several convictions. Kim Dae-jung was sentenced to death for preparing to overthrow the regime, which triggered massive protests worldwide. Thereupon he was pardoned to a long prison sentence. Two years later, he was allowed to leave for the USA.

This date, 18 May 1980, has always been remembered in South Korea. In retrospect, it is regarded as a milestone on the road to democracy. At the same time, it turned out to be problematic that US military troops were involved in the suppression of the revolt. This fact initially fostered an anti-American mood and also had an impact on the question of how to stand for reunification with North Korea, as opposing camps first emerged.

X. The 5th Republic of South Korea (1981 – 1988)

Under the leadership of Chun Doo-hwan, the 5th Republic of South Korea was established. Like Park in indirect elections, he was elected as **president** in February 1981. In addition, the National Assembly was elected and eight different parties were elected. Chun made a constitutional amendment that allowed a president to be elected for seven years but only for one term. He also abolished martial law. He promised a new era in which he would build a "**great Korea**" with economic growth and democratic principles. The judiciary would be established independently and as an authority independent of the government. The political parties might also become active again. However, since the indirect presidential election would remain in the new constitution, many high-ranking military members would receive influential positions. In addition, laws were retained that allowed opponents of the regime to be persecuted. In this respect, the 5th Republic also had an **autocratic style of rule**.

The population showed little confidence in the government with its promise of democracy. The National Assembly was re-elected in 1985, and the ruling party won fewer votes than the opposition, signaling a clear desire for a different government. Again and again, student protests flared up, and many non-academics joined them. The government took the lead over the critics. In early 1987, a student was taken into custody and died during police interrogation. As a result, the **anti-government sentiment** intensified, until in June of the same year more than a million people took part in a protest movement that advocated a democratic social order and, in particular, the direct election of the president.

Chun Doo-hwan suggested the pro-government former general **Roh Tae-Woo** as his successor (since he himself was not allowed to be re-elected). He had recognised the signs of the times and had Chun work out a program for **constitutional reforms** as his last official act. They included the direct election of the president and a reduction of his presidency to five years. In fact, Roh was (narrowly) elected in February 1988. This was surprising in that regime critics Kim Young-sam and Kim Dae-jung also took power. With this peaceful takeover, the 5th Republic came to an end.

During his reign, Chun Doo-hwan pursued the goal of promoting the economic development of his country. He achieved this with the help of measures at stable prices and low interest rates. South Korea intensified its efforts to attract investment abroad, which boosted exports. The high-tech and computer industries developed enormously. However, rapid and intensive economic growth widened the gap between the rich and lower strata. This also explained the willingness of the population to join the student protests.

In terms of foreign policy, Chun improved relations with Japan, the Soviet Union and China and also made an effort to gain North Korea. In 1985, mutual visits were even allowed to families whose members lived in the South or North because they had been torn apart by political events.

The relations with the North, however, were fundamentally clouded, with several government officials killed in 1983 during a visit to Burma (now Myanmar) in a bomb attack attributed to North Korea (most likely true but unproven). Chun himself was not injured in the attack. **Ronald Reagan**, a hardline anti-Communist, had been in power in the US since 1980. A consolidation of American relations with South Korea thus meant a greater distance to the communist North.

Chun succeeded in bringing the **1988 Olympic Summer Games** to the capital, Seoul, in which North Korea had several of its own athletes participate. He also promoted culture, e.g. he had the Korean National Museum built.

XI. The 6th Republic of South Korea

1. Roh Tae-woo (born in 1932), President from 1988 to 1993

Roh Tae-woo (born in 1932) was a former general. He succeeded in winning the presidency largely because the two opposition politicians Kim Young-sam and Kim Dae-jung were unable to agree on a candidacy and therefore both ran for the presidency, so that they took each other's votes away. In the very first year of his presidency, the Summer Olympics took place, for which his predecessor had laid the foundations and which successfully proceeded under his regency. With his politics he aspired to:

- Economic growth combined with justice

- The democratisation of the society

- Rapprochement with North Korea up to reunification

First, the universities regained their autonomy, and freedom of the press was reinstated.

The economic situation in which South Korea found itself deteriorated in this period. The strengthened trade unions fought for higher wages. This, together with the changed value of the won against the dollar, led to a drop in exports. The country's international competitiveness was impaired, especially as commodity prices rose.

Roh was very active in foreign policy. He initiated diplomatic relations with Hungary, Poland, the former Yugoslavia, Mongolia, Bulgaria and Romania. Relations with China and the Soviet Union improved, also at the trade level. Seoul and Moscow established reciprocal consulates general. During a visit to Washington, Roh met both American President George Bush and Soviet Head of State Mikhail Gorbachev.

In 1991, both South Korea and North Korea joined the United Nations.

In 1992, Roh sealed an entrance to Halla Mountain leading to the remains of the victims of the **Jeju Uprising in 1948**. In the process, left-wing activists on the island of Jeju rebelled against the right-wing regional government. The latter suppressed the uprising, killing large sections of the population in massacres. (Later a memorial was erected there.)

2. Kim Young-sam (1927 – 2015), President from 1993 to 1998

In 1990, Roh-Tae-woo and Kim Young-sam formed a political alliance that united their two parties to form a Conservative Party. This allowed Kim Young-sam to win the presidential election against Kim Dae-jung, who was also a candidate again.

Kim Young-sam wanted to reform the country. In order to be economically successful and with moral integrity, he immediately launched a **campaign against corruption**. He also wanted to draw a clear dividing line between the politics and the military, which had still not succeeded as many politicians came from the military sector. Government officials and high-ranking military officials had to disclose their sources of income and wealth. An immediate consequence was the resignation of many people from the relevant offices and positions. Kim was also making a lot of effort to reduce the concentrated power of the chaebols by reforming the law. For example, he banned anonymous bank accounts.

In 1996, the anti-corruption campaign led to the **indictment of the predecessors Chun Doo-hwan and Roh Tae-woo**, initially for bribery and later also for treason for their role in the 1979 coup and the massacre of Gwanju. Roh admitted embezzlement amounting to several million US dollars and received 17 years in prison. Chun was sentenced to death and a short time later given a life sentence. Kim Young-sam pardoned both a year after the convictions as one of his last official acts.

However, Kim Young-sam's reputation also suffered considerably because of the so-called **Hanbo scandal**. Members of the Kim government had put banks under pressure and bribed them to grant Hanbo cheap loans. The losses for South Korea were estimated at about six billion US dollars. In addition to high-ranking politicians, the sons of Kim Young-sam were also involved in the incidents and had to go to prison. That was a great humiliation for him. He apologised to the Korean people and said that he was very ashamed because he apparently had not taken enough care of his sons and felt responsible. He would have survived many difficult situations but never such a catastrophe as this.

During Kim Young-sam's tenure, devastating events occurred. It began in 1993 with a **train collision** and a **ship sinking**. In 1994, a part of the **Seongsu Bridge** suddenly broke away and 32 people lost their lives. In 1997, 228 people died during the **faulty landing approach of a Boeing** to the island of Guam. Then came the worst, the **"Asian crisis" of 1997 and 1998**. Besides Thailand and Indonesia, it mainly affected South Korea. It was an economic crisis with considerable effects on the financial market and currency stability. The chaebol group KIA belonged to the companies that were collapsing (KIA later became part of the Hyundai Kia group). The president had to call on the **International Monetary Fund for a rescue operation** worth billions.

3. Kim Dae-jung (1925 – 2009), President from 1998 to 2003

South Korea followed the democratic principles of the constitution, which since Roh Tae-woo had limited the presidential term to five years and elected the president directly. Kim Young-sam had no chance because of the corruption affair. **Kim Dae-jung** – who'd had to go into exile under the dictatorship of Park and escaped the grip of the Intelligence Service by a hair's breadth – was elected.

Kim Dae-jung saw himself in the situation of having to cope with the consequences of the economic crisis. South Korea had debts. He was succeeding in finding foreign investors and getting domestic industry back on its feet. At the beginning of 1998, he launched the equally creative and successful "**Gold Collecting**" program. Samsung, Daewoo and Hyundai set a good example by donating a lot of the precious metal to the state. At the same time, they also collected gold from the ranks of the population. An incredible solidarity movement was set in motion. Successful athletes donated their trophies, and married couples donated their rings.

It took less than three days, and the government reported **20 tons of gold worth about 100 million US dollars**. The figures, which continued to rise, were reported to the public so as not to influence the price of gold. The total value of the action was estimated at up to 200 million US dollars. For the whole of South Korea, this action had an immense symbolic effect. Everyone was convinced that the crisis had been overcome before the turn of the millennium and that everyone had contributed their own share. South Korea gained inner cohesion.

Actually, things were going uphill. The government supported the economic **development of the IT sector**. It introduced a reliable pension system, expanded educational opportunities for everyone and was also culturally active. In 1996, Kim achieved **South Korea's admission to the Organization for Economic Cooperation and Development (OECD)**. Together with Japan, his country was awarded **FIFA 2002**. North Korea refused to participate but broadcasted many matches, including South Korea's victories over Italy and Spain (before losing to Germany).

Kim Dae-jung, like his predecessor, was trying to make a move towards the North. In June 2000, **the first inter-Korean Summit** was held in Pyongyang between him and the head of the state, Kim Jong-il. Various economic initiatives and family reunification were agreed. In the same year, dozens of North Koreans could meet their relatives in the South. Kim Dae-jung was awarded the **Nobel Peace Prize** for his political commitment.

In 2001, the large and important **Incheon** Airport was opened, which strongly promoted international air traffic in South Korea.

On 29 June 2002, an **incident occurred in the Yellow Sea**. North Korean ships repeatedly crossed the border line, which ran as a buffer zone between the two divided countries but was never recognised as a border by the North. There had also been isolated incidents in this sea area in the 1990s. For example, the North Koreans had tried to smuggle a mini-submarine into South Korean waters.

A North Korean patrol boat clearly crossed the border. The South Koreans asked it to return and were fired upon. It came to a gun battle in which four South Koreans died and 19 were wounded. It is estimated that the North suffered the loss of 30 killed or wounded soldiers. The event took place during the World Cup.

While the relationship between the governments cooled down again and Kim Dae-jung spoke out clear words of warning, thousands of South Koreans showed their cohesion by putting together masses dressed in red shirts and watching the match against Turkey for third place (South Korea lost). The North Korean government never published the number of its victims in the naval battle.

4. Roh Moo-hyun (1946 to 2009), President from 2003 to 2007

Roh Moo-hyun became president in December 2002 by direct election in accordance with the constitution and formed a centre-left government. His motto was to create a "**participatory government**", which would be demanded above all by the young and bourgeois voter groups. The aim was to strengthen civil society and the less developed regions. Implementation also required **reforms in administrative activities**, whose processes slowed down considerably as a result. This was not well received by the population. In the struggle to equalise politics and business, Roh was met with opposition. The Constitutional Court, however, stopped the impeachment proceedings they had initiated against him.

Roh strengthened **reforms** oriented towards the market economy, including changes in the tax system. He continued to fight corruption. This weakened the centralist, family-run chaebols. Several of their top managers had to deal with fraud scandals. Large corporations had to disclose their financial actions and searched their records, including Samsung and parts of Hyun-dai.

This created a sentiment against Roh in these economic circles. There were loud doubts as to whether it would not cause an economic down-turn. The critics of the giant companies, on the other hand, argued that it would be impossible to use anything from an air conditioner to a pas-senger train without chaebols being involved, which, however, accounted for only 4% of jobs and only about 12% of economic growth. There was also criticism of the spirit with which the founding families competed with each other for the greatest assets instead of focusing their businesses on profits. **Daewoo**'s boss was im-prisoned for his role in the collapse of his busi-ness and illegal appropriation of billions of dol-lars, as was **Hyundai**'s boss for embezzlement. Despite many successes, the unemployment rate remained high, especially among young people, and unrest in businesses continued.

In 2005, South Korea was shocked by the fact that its highly acclaimed **stem cell researcher Hwang Woo-Suk**, who had announced the cloning of an extinct Siberian lion among other things, had been exposed as a counterfeiter; but in 2006, there was great joy in the appointment of **Foreign Minister Ban Ki-moon as general secretary of the United Nations**.

Roh pursued the policy of greater independence from America and further understanding with North Korea. In 2003, several hundred South Koreans traveled to Pyongyang to open a sports hall sponsored by Hyundai. The mass crossing of the demilitarised zone was a historic event.

In 2007 **the second inter-Korean Summit** took place, between Roh and Kim Jong-il. They talked about peace negotiations, but the status quo of the official ceasefire remained unchanged. They signed cooperation agreements.

In the same year it came to a historically significant event. Roh granted North Korea economic aid amounting to 80 million US dollars. Many North Koreans were working in the **Kaesong industrial complex**, a special economic zone in South Korea, as a result of economic cooperation between the two Korean states. The conditions here were particularly favourable for company founders, and the jobs were filled jointly by North and South Korea.

Two trains crossed the border, one from North to South with destination Kaesong and one in the other direction. It was more than half a century ago that such train encounters were possible from both parts of the peninsula. There were 150 passengers in each train, including politicians. In South Korea they waved "reunification flags" and let balloons fly. In the compartments of the North Korean train there were conductors in military uniforms; on the outside it said, "In this train the great President Kim Il-sung already drove."

This encounter was essentially symbolic and did not repeat itself, especially as North Korea had only agreed to this one trip. But Roh continued his policy of rapprochement. For example, he had landmines removed from the border strip. At the same time he started talks with America about a free trade agreement, but these were protracted.

During Roh's reign there was a **conflict with Japan**. In 2005, South Korea complained of

Japan's presence on the **Liancourt cliffs**. This was the internationally used neutral name for the archipelago, called Dokdo by South Korea and Tadeshima by Japan. The area enriched with fish and (most likely) mineral resources had been controversially discussed between the two countries, the affiliation remained unclear. South Korea has administered this region since 1945. The event clouded the improved relations with Japan, also from an economic point of view. South Korean newspapers reported that citizens set themselves on fire out of rage over Japan and a desperate citizen even jumped off a bridge. Some demonstrators claimed that the danger presented by Japan was greater than that presented by North Korea; here the memories of old colonial times were brought back to life.

But Roh's behaviour towards North Korea, in addition to dissatisfaction with the lack of economic growth, was what disturbed many South Koreans. In 2007, they voted Roh out of office.

Then Roh was **suspected of corruption**. In 2009, he admitted that his wife and other family members had received approximately $6 million from a businessman during his tenure. However, he asserted that he knew nothing about it and that his wife had paid off debts with it. Nevertheless, he apologised to the people through the press for disappointing them. In May, he committed **suicide** by jumping off rocky cliffs. In his farewell letter to his family he wrote (analogously), "Don't be sad, life and death belong to nature. I am not sorry. No one is to blame, it is destiny."

5. The Sunshine Policy of South Korea

The term "Sunshine Policy" was derived from an Aesop fable. Sun and wind argued about their strength. As winners, they wanted to recognise who first persuaded a wanderer to take off his coat. The stronger the wind blew, the more the chosen person clung to his coat, but the friendly rays of the sun caused him to take it off. The moral was that gentle action is stronger than violence.

The policy that Park Chung-hee had already started towards North Korea and which Kim Dae-jung and Roh Moo-hyun consistently pursued was called the **Sunshine Policy** because it was based on a fundamentally peaceful, approaching and cooperative attitude towards the North and definitely did not want to initiate any hostilities without abandoning a willingness to defend. It contained **three firm principles**:

1. An armed provocation by North Korea was not tolerated.

2. South Korea did not seek to integrate North Korea into the South in any way.

3. South Korea actively sought cooperation.

Kim Young-sam, in particular, assumed that a rapid change in the tendency towards hostility was not to be expected in Pyongyang and geared himself towards a long-term strategy. The fact that he provided financial aid to North Korea on the basis of his plans was then interpreted as corruption and treason at the end of his term of office

South Korea supported **the development of infrastructure in North Korea**, for example the construction and repair of roads. The companies in the South were subsidised if they co-operated with the North. There were a few dozen contracts that ensured that companies were active in or for North Korea, from mining and tourism to manufacturing, e.g. in the car industry. A shining example was the cooperation between the two states in the **Kaesong industrial plant**, in the heyday of which some 50,000 North Koreans worked for South Korean companies.

The aim of the Sunshine Policy was to **raise the standard of living in the North** (which was meanwhile much higher than in the South), which of course also encouraged the tendency for the North to depend more and more on its southern counterpart. There were also South Korean companies that introduced a **social component**, for example ensuring that every North Korean child could drink a portion of milk with a meal a day.

However, it turned out again and again that there was a lot of mistrust between South and

North Korean businessmen. Everyone would have done business with a partner from a third country rather than with the "other" Korea. This delayed the development of trade. The South Koreans were constantly afraid of being cheated and of not receiving decent goods; while the North Koreans believed that the South still had a hidden strategy behind all these contracts to one day insidiously annex the North.

During the Sunshine Policy there were numerous **contacts between the South and North Koreans**. The demilitarised zone, which for security reasons included two kilometers of no-man's-land on each side, experienced heavy border traffic. Above all, families torn apart could meet. But also many NGOs (non-governmental organisations) finally took a look at North Korea, and tourists admired the natural highlight Kumgang, an extraordinarily beautiful mountain region. The North Koreans were struck by the good physical condition and high-quality clothing of the South Koreans, which clearly showed their prosperity compared to the much poorer conditions in the North.

Several hundred thousand soldiers were stationed in the 240-kilometer demilitarised zone. The monitoring center and common security zone for both sides was located in the **ceasefire site Panmunjeom**. Since the end of the Korean War, the north had used huge loudspeaker systems to sound the South from the DMZ, with battle music and eulogies about its head of state. The South reacted with Korean folk songs and lectures on freedom and democracy. A consequence of the Sunshine Policy in 2004 was that both sides stopped these mutual provocations.

One of the positive results of the policy was **economic development for both sides**. Although South Korea bore a large financial burden and contributed a great deal of know-how and capital, it achieved increased economic stability and the confidence of foreign investors and markets.

The negative side was that critics viewed the financial efforts as **aid for North Korea's nuclear program** and argued that most of the money had not gone to the population but to the regime's weapons system.

6. Lee Myung-bak (born in 1941), President from 2008 to the end of 2012

After Roh Moo-hyun's suicide, **Lee Myung-bak** was elected as a president. He was a member of the Conservative Party, replacing the centre-left social-liberal government. He had political experience. During his student days, he took part in protests against government policies and was imprisoned. He was later elected to the National Assembly, after which he held the office of **mayor of Seoul**. But he also had business experience, having spent many years as **Hyundai's managing director** before his political career. Here he acquired the nickname "**Bulldozer**" because of his energetic approach.

Lee promoted the development of a market economy and strengthened state power; he introduced **student loans** in the education sector. Immediately after his election, he reopened the market for beef imports from the USA. Thus he lost popularity among the population who were afraid of the rampant mad cow disease. In the years that followed, he succeeded in stabilising the economic situation that had been stricken by the **global financial crisis in 2008/09**. In 2011, he ratified the **free trade agreement with the USA** that Roh had initiated.

In the first year of his presidency, the country suffered a depressing accident. An arsonist has set fire to the prestigious national treasure market, the Namdaemuntor in Seoul. The roof had to be completely renewed. The cost of the repair, which would take years, was estimated to be at least 20 million US dollars.

Lee was a declared **opponent of the Sunshine Policy**. Believing that the North received far more help (e.g. staple foods such as rice) than it gave back in return (which was the calculated basic feature of this kind of policy), he wanted to end it. **North Korea, with Kim Jong-il** at the helm, had so far allowed individual cooperation but had never abandoned its fundamentally negative stance. For example, he continued to deny that hundreds of (now old) prisoners of war and kidnapped fishermen from the Korean War still lived there and were not permitted to return. Lee also disturbed North Korea's persistent work on the nuclear program.

Lee stopped the generous practice of his predecessors that South Korean companies could settle in the North. North Korea then expelled several South Korean politicians from the joint Kaesong industrial complex. The northern country thereupon presented itself as independent from the South and did not ask for any support. It also feared further UN resolutions against it. In 2006, for example, a resolution was passed allowing North Korean freight transports to be controlled because of the nuclear weapons tests.

In 2010, Kim Jong-il accepted South Korean aid supplies again, especially as food was running short. Lee followed the line of receiving **humanitarian aid for the population but remaining politically tough**. A year earlier, North Korea had cancelled all agreements with the South; however, when Kim Dae-jung died, it sent a high-ranking delegation to pay tribute to the late ex-president.

In the same year, the **spectacular sinking of a South Korean naval ship** took place. The *Cheonan* was located in the controversial territorial waters between the South Korean and North Korean borders. It was torpedoed and went up in flames, 46 crew members died. A commission of inquiry found the torpedo steering of the type used by North Korea. At the same time, some small submarines had also entered the area from a northern base. A commission of experts from Western countries, which was called in, came to the conclusion that North Korea was responsible for the incident. But the local government denied any involvement.

Lee stopped all trade with North Korea. Kim Jong-il, for his part, broke off all diplomatic relations with the South on the basis that the evidence of the shipwreck was fictitious. Then there was a **collision on the South Korean island Yeonpyeong**. The South Korean military, together with American soldiers, held a maneuver and fired into the sea, where nobody was endangered. But North Korea opened fire against the island and hit military and civilian targets. South Korea fired back. North Korea had one killed and one injured soldier to mourn; the South had two dead and 16 wounded soldiers as well as three dead civilians.

Lee Myung-bak drafted a plan for policy with North Korea. His goal was **reunification**, to which three stages led:

- An economic community

- A peace community

- A reunification tax

He wanted to "**abolish the wall of different systems and form a community of the Korean nation**" and called for "**coexistence instead of confrontation and progress instead of stagnation.**" He saw **North Korea's nuclear disarmament** as the first, indispensable prerequisite. At the same time he warned the country against aggression.

The general staff of the North Korean People's Army threatened that it would give a merciless answer in renewed military manoeuvres, as on Yeonpyeong. But South Korea, together with the USA, held the annual joint maneuver, which involved over 80,000 soldiers. The North neither attacked nor disarmed.

Two years later, Lee agreed with **US President Barack Obama** to respond to Kim Jong-il's armament and ongoing tensions with a missile system stationed in South Korea and extended to 800 kilometers in range.

At the end of 2010, Seoul was the venue for the **G20 Summit**. In view of the global crisis, the participants agreed on stricter regulations for banks.

In 2012, Lee Myung-bak was the **first South Korean president to show himself on the Liancourt cliffs**. On the main island, he had himself filmed by television crews, to Japan's annoyance, in front of a group of rocks on which "ROK Territory" stood (ROK is the abbreviation for "Republic of Korea", the official name of South Korea). He emphasised that the archipelago belonged to South Korea and must be protected.

In October 2018, long after his term in office, Lee was charged **with serious crimes** and sentenced to 15 years in prison and approximately 10 million euros (converted). He lodged an appeal. The charges were bribery and embezzlement. Among other things, he was supposed to own the company DAS, which he claimed was owned by his brother. With money from the company he was said to have given bribes in the millions. He was also alleged to have ordered the pardon of a Samsung CEO, who was threatened with a heavy fine for tax offences, in exchange for bribes.

7. Park Geun-hyu (born in 1952) President from 2013 to 2017

Shortly before Christmas 2012, **Park Geun-hyu** won the regular presidential elections and was sworn in by February 2013.

Park brought a personally heavy legacy with her. When she was 22 years old, her mother was shot by an assassin who had wanted to meet her father. As a result, she was pushed into the role of first lady, barely grown up. Five years later, her father, President Park Chung-hee, was shot by his own intelligence service. Like a shadow, she stood behind her actions. Whatever she decided was often judged in connection with her. Some saw the former head of state as an arbitrary dictator, others as the shining hero of the country. Park Geun-hyu, as an election campaigner, was also the **victim of an assassin** who attacked her with a knife in 2006, but the outcome was mild. For many years she was **chairman of the conservative Saenuri Party**, to which Lee Myung-bak also belonged. She was inferior to him at the last presidential constellation within the party.

Park proclaimed her domestic mission to focus more on the people than on the nation. She wanted to create "**a happy life for all**" and a "**culture of coexistence and prosperity.**" This proved to be no easy task, if only because youth unemployment was high and in the course of her political work she would not succeed in reducing it noticeably.

First, she restructured both the government offices and the administration. There were **new ministers, for example for science, for information and communication technology and for fisheries**. She wanted the average population to be able to make a good living. One step in this direction was the **free trade**

agreement with Australia, which she signed in 2014.

Park was committed to the elimination of social grievances. She also pointed to growing domestic and sexual violence and a higher propensity to violence in schools. For this reason, she founded a committee to counteract this. In 2013, on the anniversary of the massacre of Gwangju, she spoke and expressed her sympathy to the relatives.

As the first foreign policy action, Park visited American **President Barack Obama** and intensified relations with the USA. Both made a statement in which they emphasised the good relationship between the two states. With their cooperation they wanted to promote peace in North-East Asia. More than 20,000 GIs were stationed in South Korea. They also wanted to expand their trade relations with Park insisting on better promotion of South Korean science and technology know-how by American experts.

Park was the first South Korean head of state to visit Iran under **Ayatollah Ruhollah Khomenei**, with whom she agreed more cooperation and increased trade. She talked to Russian President **Vladimir Putin** in 2013 during the G20 Summit and later during his visit to South Korea. They spoke about economic cooperation and support in the policy towards North Korea, especially in the so-called six-party talks.

The **six-party talks** dealt with how to deal with North Korea's nuclear weapons development. The participants were China, Russia, Japan and the USA. Park wanted to achieve greater influence. But the talks were already sluggish, and North Korea stopped them in 2009.

Park presented the active foreign policy of her predecessors and visited several states, including Germany. South Korea was taking an increasingly important place in the world community, while North Korea was isolating itself more and more.

However, there were always problems with **Japan**, especially because of the Liancourt rocks but also because of the "**comfort women**". This was the Japanese name for forced prostitutes in Japanese wartime brothels, who came from South Korea, among other places. After a hard struggle, Park's foreign minister achieved that Japan paid about 7.5 million euros (converted) into a compensation fund. But the affected women and other parts of the population were dissatisfied because in their eyes the government acted autocratically without any consultation with the women. They saw the fund only as a benevolent donation but not as real compensation.

There were also differences of opinion with **China**. In 2013, both the Chinese and the South Koreans declared the expansion of the **flight control zone over the Socotra Rock in the Yellow Sea**, which became visible at low tide. Contrary to international maritime law, which did not allow any nation to claim it because of the distance from the territorial sea, both states insisted that it belonged to their territory.

In relation to **North Korea**, Park also took the view that one had to strive for reunification and could not maintain this "state of abnormality" as normality. Freedom and human rights should apply to all Koreans. She was also developing a **three-stage plan**. After a peaceful unification, economic and then political integration should take place. Due to the support of the United Nations in this attitude, North Korea initially stopped its verbal threats and military border provocations. There was also a new cooperation in the Kaesong industrial complex, which North Korea temporarily boycotted.

But all South Korean proposals envisaged **nuclear disarmament** in return for contacts and material aid packages. And the head of state, **Kim Jong-un**, who had been in office since the end of 2011, did not agree to this any more than his father Kim Jong-il did. In 2016, South Korea, for its part, ended its cooperation in Kaesong because of a North Korean nuclear weapons test. (At the beginning of 2019 Kim Jong-un talked about a resumption of the cooperation.)

In 2012 and 2013 respectively, both Korean states launched their own **satellites** into orbit. In the following years, South Korea accused the North several times of carrying out **cyberattacks**.

In the next few years, new **provocations** took place in the border regions (on land and at sea).

North Korea reacted aggressively to the extensive South Korean-American military exercises, which were taking place with increased troops in the South, and also to the hot-air balloons with attached writings against their head of state, who let South Korean activists fly from the border with the northern territory. The South resumed its border sounding with freedom and democracy texts, whereupon the loudspeakers were fired upon from the North. But there was no talk of the dead and wounded.

The year 2014 brought a catastrophe for Park and, as a result, minus points for the population, from which she never fully recovered again. The **ferry "Sevol"** capsized in the Yellow Sea. Most of the 304 victims were students. Nine passengers remained lost; their bodies were not found despite extensive search work. At a memorial service, a mother said that one should never forget that "there were still people in the rusty and stinking wreck."

The captain was convicted of murder. However, the causes of the accident were not only seen in overloading and lack of maintenance but also in excessively **lax legal regulations**. The population also blamed Park for not expressing herself publicly until seven hours after the accident. Since it was known that she was receiving beauty treatments, there was a rumour that she had done so during the same period. She stated that she had spent the time in exchange with the authorities on post-disaster measures. But mistrust was sown.

From then on, Park was increasingly accused of not being successful in economic policy, of not sufficiently respecting freedom of expression and of beautifying the state-controlled history books with regard to her father's political role. The approval of her policies was immense, even within her own party, which accused her of arbitrary decisions.

Protest rallies and demonstrations against Park took place at the end of 2016. The main reason for this was allegations of fraud and abuse of power. It was all about her **advisor Choi Soon-sil**, the daughter of a long-time confidante. She was said to have given her insights into the government's work, which must be treated as strictly confidential. Choi was said to have exploited her proximity to the president to gain considerable illegal influence on businesses. One spoke of blackmail and mailbox companies, also the name **Samsung** was mentioned. In fact, a leading member of the company was arrested and sentenced to five years in prison. Choi was also said to have forged documents to give her daughter advantages. She was sentenced to 20 years in prison. Politicians were also arrested for blacklisting regime critics, especially artists.

In December 2016, parliament requested that Park be removed from office. This was granted by the competent court. In 2017, she was arrested and in 2018, mainly for **bribery**, sentenced to 25 years in prison and (converted) 15 million euros in fines. In an independent trial, she was also sentenced to eight years in prison for **accepting funds from the intelligence service and illegally influencing the election**.

XII. North Korea

1. Kim Il-sung (1919 – 1994), Dictator from 1948 to 1994

In 1948, **Kim Il-sung** took over governmental power in the newly founded Democratic People's Republic. A year later, he also secured the **leadership of the Workers' Party**. He nipped all opposition parties and movements in the bud or suspended them. **Purges**, which eliminated critics of the regime, also ran through his entire period of rule. He had previously served as a major in the army of the Soviet Union. Under his **Stalinist leadership**, North Korea entered the Korean War.

His goals were **economic strengthening** under the supremacy of the state and **abolition of private property**, advancement of the industrial branches as well as a **reunification** with the South under his leadership and the power of government of the North. He agreed a summit with South Korea's President Kim Young-Sam in 1994, which was historically significant but failed because he himself had died before. He was given the nickname "**the eternal president**" throughout his life.

Immediately after the Korean War and until the end of the 1960s, North Korea's economy stabilised, mainly with the help of the **Soviet Union**. But then things went rapidly downhill. In the 1990s, **famines** occurred as a result of mismanagement, especially in agriculture. When weather catastrophes occurred, the country had nothing more to offer against the considerable loss of harvests. Stocks were quickly depleted.

The **collapse of the Soviet Union** at the beginning of the 1990s and the lack of support from a like-minded partner were added to this. The life quality of the population dropped enormously. Until shortly before the turn of the millennium, almost **a million people starved to death in North Korea**. Those who could stay afloat suffered privations. Even the average size of young people was decreasing, so that military uniforms had to be cut smaller. Many people fled to neighbouring China or the South. Some reported that Chinese pets received better food than people in their home country.

Kim Il-sung established a system of **militarisation, state domination, deprivatisation and absolute control**. The state took over the supervision of the media. He was the owner of every product, from shops where you could buy material things to the intellectual property of ideas and thoughts that could be expressed in human communities and organisations. The right to travel was also severely restricted.

In order to ideologically substantiate his politics (of oppression), Kim Il-sung drafted a theory that he wanted to be understood as a further development of Marxism-Leninism, tailored to Korea. It was titled "**Juche**" (English: independence) and was based on the following points.

1. Economic self-sufficiency and independence from other states

2. North Korea's unconditional ability to defend itself

3. The political sovereignty of North Korea

Above all, he justified the strong build-up of the military and the constant presence of soldiers throughout the country with this. He propagated his ideas as the (analogously) "revolutionary spirit of his own strength", but outsiders saw them as a compulsion to unconditional obedience to the Communist Party.

Kim Il-sung strengthened his rule with a social system, which he introduced at the end of the '50s and which was called **songbun**. The North Korean people found themselves in five groups, the first of which was the best and the fifth was the worst. The classification was based on two criteria.

The first was to determine the political position of the ancestors on their father's side, which went back several generations. Anyone who was on Kim Il-sung's side early on produced (often posthumously) the best songbun for his descendants; opponents did the opposite.

The second related to the current profession. However, there was one component that exceeded professional status. Once you'd been in contact with Kim Il-sung, you would increase your songbun enormously. Therefore, it was highly coveted to be photographed with him when he was in the public eye. Thus, a part of the pictures was created that showed cheering crowds. If you could prove that you talked to him for at least a quarter of an hour, you could also put this on the credit side of your songbun.

Songbun has had an effect on the life of every individual since early youth. It depended on which school you were allowed to go to and where you lived. If you had a dissident in your family, you would probably never live in the capital; you would probably not even be allowed to visit it. Inhabitants of Pyongyang with a bad songbun had to resettle in unattractive border areas. The (North Korean) world was also open to anyone close to Kim. Excluded from the songbun was the allocation of food, which was made dependent on the workplace.

Anyone who spoke out against the system committed a serious crime. He was imprisoned or sentenced to death in a camp for political prisoners. Family members up to the third generation could also be punished, mostly with imprisonment in camps. Many executions took place in public. The closest relatives were forced to sit in the front row. Schools closed on that day because the students had to attend the execution. At the same time, children were instructed to observe their parents and neighbours were told to keep an eye on one another. The door was opened for **denunciation**.

All these measures were applied more or less sharply throughout this and subsequent dictatorships in North Korea. Only the songbun of origin was somewhat softened because parts of the civil service protested vehemently against atoning for the sins of their ancestors. North Korea fundamentally denied the existence of camps as shown, for example, by American aerial photographs.

2. Kim Jong-il (1941 – 2011), Dictator from 1994 to 2011

Kim Jong-il studied economics in Pyongyang after going to school both in the former GDR and in China. Already at the age of 23, he was given a leading position in the Labour Party and from then on was in fact a politician. Among other things, he acted as private secretary for his own father, whose successor he had already been appointed in 1980. Nevertheless, before Kim Il-sung's death he hardly appeared in public.

He did, however, handle orders such as the **kidnappings** typical of North Korea. He arranged for the kidnapping of a respected director and a renowned actress from South Korea. They had to make several films for the fanatical cinema fan (including the character Godzilla) before they were allowed to return home after several years. Japanese, Malay, Thai, French and other foreigners are also kidnapped. They were to pass on their know-how to North Korea. The foreign minister at that time, **Madeleine Albright**, found that Kim Jong-il acted far beyond the powers of his office.

Kim Jong-il was considered a strange, almost mysterious personality. The South Korean media often showed him as a pompous character, who liked to lead a Playboy life with lots of culinary delights and in female company. Russian ambassadors reported that he drank a lot of wine and ate lobster with silver chopsticks. But in political circles he was regarded as **intelligent, well-informed and manipulative**.

He continued the propaganda actions of his father even more massively and he let himself be worshipped as a hero. A real **personality cult** was developed. It was said that when he was born on a holy mountain a double rainbow and a super bright star appeared in the sky—which was predicted. However, it was very likely that he saw the light of the world in a Soviet military base.

During Kim's reign, the domestic political crisis worsened by another **famine**. Fuels for factories and energy for heated offices were running out. While he continued to isolate his country from foreign policy, he asked China for help. At the same time he suppressed emerging unrest and strengthened the military presence. He arrested two American journalists for political reasons.

The president of the USA, **Bill Clinton**, personally achieved their release. The crime rate and prostitution increased among the population due to the difficult conditions. People were trying to turn everything into money in order to get food. Those who could flee did so, especially to China.

After the turn of the millennium, the **economy eased**. Markets for goods and services were more tolerated; there was a low level of private enterprise. China strengthened its trade relations with North Korea. The joint Korean **industrial complex Kaesong** provided work and bread. But Kim mistrusted every anti-communist tendency and started a currency reform to destroy private property. When this led to inflation, the regime became more or less friendly with a low level of private initiative.

Kim Jong-il was temporarily concerned to ease tensions with South Korea, as the summit with President Kim Dae-jung in 2000 showed. A few years later, he transferred about 50 million US dollars to North Korea as aid for a **flood disaster**. Kim Il-jung then released some South Korean fishermen. He sent a delegation to commemorate the death of the South Korean head of state.

Kim Jong-il died in December 2011. The death of the ruler was accompanied by immense public mourning. The myths about his person flared up again, spread by the state-controlled media. They reported unbelievable natural phenomena that were said to have occurred at death, such as the sudden break-up of an icy lake, the red glow of the sacred mountain on which he was said to have been born, and a mass gathering of magpies gathered in a tree to mourn.

The subliminal remorse was activated among the population, which was constantly kept alive because Kim was always portrayed as an ex-tremely hard-working man who did superhuman things for his people and whom everyone should emulate. At times he was almost worshipped as a god. He was said to have walked at the age of three weeks and never had to go to the toilet. Under his guidance he received more than 30 glorifying names, e.g. "the dear leader". Instead of "dear" also "unique", "brilliant" and "great" were used. Other names were "Sun of the Communist Future", "Shining Star of Mount Paektu" (the alleged birth mountain), and "Be-loved Father".

3. Kim Jong-un (born in 1983 or 1984), Chief Leader since 2011

Already in 2009 Kim Jong-il had made his youngest son **Kim Jong-un** the supreme commander of the intelligence service. In the autumn of the following year, he appointed him to senior political positions and entrusted him with important military duties. It was therefore not surprising that he **was appointed leader of the party, army and state** immediately after his father's death. The "Chief Leader", as he is officially called, went to school in Switzerland and then attended the military university in Pyongyang. In all probability, he never did military service.

After taking over his position of power Kim Jong-un was called a **"big successor"** in the country. He presents himself as a contemporary variant of his famous grandfather. As has been customary in North Korea for the ruler since his father, a picture or statue of him can be found at every turn in towns and in the countryside.

He has continued the **dictatorial policy** of removing people who do not support his policy or who could become dangerous to him and has dismissed several officials. He also does not shy away from drastic measures. To secure his power, he has executed his uncle. There was also a deadly attack on his half-brother, most likely ordered by him. He has increased the military presence at the border, resulting in a noticeable reduction in the number of refugees. He allowed the economy to shift towards market activities. He boycotted the Kaesong industrial complex for a while in April 2013, but after a few months he agreed to open it up again.

His **foreign policy style** is characterised by the fact that he oscillates between the expressed desire for a détente with South Korea and the USA, which necessarily includes the dismantling of the nuclear weapons program and anti-Americanism as well as an insistence on nuclear weapons.

4. Life in North Korea

Although the communist system has opened itself to some standards of the market economy, it has essentially acted the same in social terms for decades. This is apparent from reports by refugees and journalists who have been able to visit North Korea, as well as from reports from entrepreneurs who have worked there, and also from unnoticed records and images.

The extreme personality cult of the ruler is cultivated. The image of Kim Jong-un can be found everywhere. Also there are pictures of **rockets and weapons**, which are presented in huge size. In addition, there are **anti-American writings** that brand the USA as the great enemy. There is a museum of the Korean War that every student must visit at least once, the "**Museum about Victory in the Patriotic War**" in Pyongyang. Foreign visitors also have to stop here during their guided tours. There one is shown cruel pictures depicting the American and South Korean soldiers as inhuman and the North Korean soldiers as heroes as well as the population of North Korea as victims. The impression that the South started the war is also maintained.

Further visits lead to large agricultural facilities, where you do not come into contact with the workers. It is generally insisted that visitors have no points of contact with the population. The **Internet** is largely inaccessible. An e-mail can be sent at some hotel receptions, but it is not possible to operate a PC independently, so a check of the content is likely.

The children are educated in the belief that North Koreans are something like a **chosen people** who are doing very well but who are constantly threatened by the hostile Americans, so that they need an almost supernatural powerful leader and an effective, functioning weapons system. Students and guests from abroad are assured that North Korea is home to the happiest man in the world with the best of all leaders. Everyone, big and small, is isolated from the outside world. Mutual social control is in great demand, which leads to denunciations. Often there are **clans**. When someone is arrested for an offence, his family suddenly disappears from the scene.

The **military** has a size of about one soldier per 25 people (the USA per 230 people). This means that many soldiers are farmers who have to serve in the army. Therefore, you can regularly see people in uniforms working in the fields or building houses and roads. They are constantly present in public life. Men have to do 10 years of military service; women have to do only two.

The adequate **nutrition of the population** always remains a sore point in North Korea. The rulers have long known that they live in frenzy, while the inhabitants hardly have enough to eat. As soon as a poor harvest occurs, hunger threatens in large areas. The last time this happened was in 2016, even though North Korea's economy was growing. Large sums are constantly being invested in weapons systems.

A **bridge to China** serves to secure the most necessary things. It only exists unofficially, but nobody intervenes. Here an exchange of goods takes place, which serves the livelihood of many people and opens the door to smuggling. North Korea also has agreements with **Russia and China**. Both countries provide jobs for North Koreans, the Chinese mainly in the textile industry and the Russians mainly in forestry. However, the accounts are settled with the North Korean government, which retains up to 80% of the wages. The money goes directly to senior government officials and, of course, to the dictator himself. Without these food sources, the population would starve and freeze because the sanctions against isolated North Korea, which carries out missile and nuclear tests, have been on the increase since the turn of the millennium.

5. North Korean Missiles and Nuclear Weapons

The history of North Korea since the 1980s has been closely linked to the question of how the country has the **capacity to produce atomic bombs** and how it deals with them. The rulers of North Korea fluctuate between concessions and threats, especially to America and South Korea. At the same time, the issue of **reunification** is also being raised again and again, but despite some talks between the respective heads of state, this is becoming less and less likely as the years go by.

However, the threats of both countries to collect the other's money are steadily decreasing. Sometimes Kim Jong-un puts the threat of annihilation in place. North Korea never liked the fact that there are US army bases in South Korea, especially since it built up the image of America as an original enemy and never dismantled it. Especially under Kim Jong-un there is a constant struggle between power demonstrations and concessions.

In 1985, North Korea joined the **International Treaty on the Non-Proliferation of Nuclear Weapons** and agreed not to manufacture any nuclear weapons. However, this only happened because the American intelligence service discovered a North Korean reactor that could produce plutonium. A year later, North Korea started operating a **research nuclear reactor in Nyongbyon**, where nuclear facilities had already been built in the 1960s with Soviet assistance.

In the early 1990s, the **United Nations International Atomic Energy Agency** accused the country of not complying with the Nuclear Non-Proliferation Treaty. This suspicion arose from the authority's measurements and was reinforced because North Korea did not grant unrestricted access to the facilities. The authority assumed a nuclear potential of an estimated three warheads, which led to considerable tensions between the USA and uncooperative North Korea. Kim Jong-un threatened to terminate the contract and had a missile tested that would be fired into the Sea of Japan.

In **1994**, the escalation of tension led to a situation that almost triggered a **war**. The American President **Bill Clinton** was seriously considering a military attack on North Korea. South Korean President **Kim Young-sam** was countering this idea as best he could. But Carter was already getting support from his military advisers. At the last minute, Former President **Jimmy Carter**, known for his diplomatic skills, saved the day. He reminded the ruler **Kim Il-sung** of an invitation from earlier times.

In fact, he was allowed to enter the country (and was the first to cross the demilitarised zone on both sides in his homeland). Camouflaged as a private visit, together with his wife, Carter rewrote the **crisis management** meeting. He publicly criticised, among other things, the American government and showed himself in media-effective photos in close harmony with the North Korean dictator. In this way, the dictator could maintain his prestige and promise not to terminate the Nuclear Non-Proliferation Treaty and postpone his nuclear program for the time being. He also granted the nuclear authority unrestricted access. In return, the USA promised measures to enable the conversion of nuclear reactors to civil nuclear energy. The official negotiations began in July and Kim Il-sung died shortly afterwards. But his son brought the talks to an end in October, which went down in the history of the two states as the "**Agreed Framework**". Carter thus averted the danger of a war between North and South Korea that could easily have become a world war between great powers.

But after signing the contract, **North Korea did not behave cooperatively at all**. In 1996, it even announced that it no longer regarded the ceasefire as real and stationed thousands of additional soldiers in the demilitarised zone. Two years later, it fired a long-range missile over Japan, which landed in the Pacific.

After the terrorist attacks on the World Trade Center in September 2001, **George W. Bush**, who became the president that year and favored a tough stance towards North Korea anyway, drew a red line to "**rogue states**" and an "**Axis of Evil**". He counted North Korea among both, which he also named as a possible target for the use of nuclear weapons. This attitude reinforced the tendency that behind South Korea stood the

USA and behind North Korea, which, since the collapse of the Soviet Union, could no longer count on Russia's unconditional support, more and more was China.

The situation was getting worse again. At the end of 2002 it became known that North Korea had a **nuclear program** based on uranium, including in Nyongbyon. A few months later, Kim Jong-il again announced the withdrawal from the Nuclear Non-Proliferation Treaty and boycotted the surveillance of the UN authority by deporting the inspectors and having the surveillance cameras destroyed. As a result, the USA, Japan and South Korea stopped oil supplies to his country in a joint agreement.

In 2005, Kim Jong-il announced that he possessed **nuclear weapons**, which North Korea needed for self-defense, especially against the "imperialist state USA." Experts have estimated the available material to be sufficient to build up to six atomic bombs. One year later, he had **underground nuclear tests** carried out, which were strongly condemned by the international community. Once again, economic sanctions were imposed, supported by the UN.

In 2007, there was a **temporary easing** of tension because North Korea shut down its reactor in Nyongbyon and granted access to the control bodies, for which it received several ten thousand tons of heating oil as an aid measure. The word "**peace treaty**" was also used.

But, just two years later, the North Korean ruler abandoned all cooperation and tested a long-range rocket. The main reasons for the change of sentiment were Japanese economic sanctions and the trend reversal in North Korea policy by the new South Korean President Lee Myung-bak. The second **underground nuclear test** followed in 2009.

When **Kim Jong-un**'s reign began, the basic conditions in North Korea remained unchanged. After one year, the new ruler spread the news that his missiles could easily reach the USA. This was probably a reaction to an agreement between America and South Korea in which an increase in the range of South Korean missiles was noted. In 2012, North Korea failed a missile launch, which was supposed to bring a **satellite** into orbit (allegedly to commemorate Kim Il-sung's 100th birthday). In fact, however, this project still succeeded in a second attempt.

During Kim Jong-un's reign, the **nuclear test number three fell in 2013**. The UN Security Council again imposed sanctions. This time China also intervened with criticism of North Korea. In the same year, a North Korean ship was discovered in Panama hiding jet fighters under sugar sacks. Kim Jong-un also threatened with first **nuclear strikes** against the two countries on the occasion of the annual joint military exercises of America and South Korea and announced a few months later that the Nyongbyon nuclear power plant was fully activated. He also closed the Kaesong industrial center to North Koreans. The world public was talking about another "**Korean crisis**".

At the beginning of 2016, Kim Jong-un referred to the successful test of a **hydrogen bomb**. Experts doubted this because the media only show a container that did not necessarily have to contain a bomb. But then the ruler reported on his **nuclear tests number four and five**, which in turn were followed by UN sanctions.

This time it was decided to buy far less coal and minerals from North Korea (less than 50%).

North Korea has contacts with Pakistan, Iran and other countries. It is assumed that they exchange materials, plans and programs for weapons and atomic systems; North Korea itself exports technical accessories for missile construction to these countries, among other things. North Korea's declared goal, as the regime itself proclaims, is to have nuclear warheads that can reach the US through an **intercontinental missile**. Kim Jong-un declared in 2017 that this goal had been achieved.

XIII. Developments in 2017 and 2018

1. Elections in South Korea

In the May 2017 elections, Park's Conservative Party had no chance. The candidate of the centre-left party Minju, **Moon Jae-in (born in 1953)**, became president with an overwhelming majority. His parents had fled the Korean War from the North.

In the 2012 election, Moon was the opponent to Park Geun-Hye, which won by a narrow margin. He remained politically active and quickly became the top man in the candidate competition after Park's removal from office. His strong competitor from the Conservative Party was **Ban Ki-moon**, the former general secretary of the United Nations, who announced his withdrawal shortly before the election.

Moon started with a promise to limit the **power of the chaebols**, who still had a strong influence. In connection with this, he wanted to fight the links between government and industry. In

North Korea's policy, he was pursuing the goal of achieving a diplomatic solution in the sense of an understanding. His critics immediately described this attitude as an inappropriate new sunshine policy.

2. Relationship between South Korea and North Korea

North Korea was testing a ballistic missile a few days after Moon took power. He responded with a series of live fire exercises conducted by South Korean soldiers together with GIs. When the North shot a long-range missile into the Sea of Japan in July, Moon referred to his cooperation with the US and stressed that, despite his unshakable belief in dialogue he considered it necessary to defend his country competently.

A month later, Kim Jong-un threatened to launch missiles into the Pacific near the **island of Guam**, where an American military base was stationed. It was to be wrapped in a "historical fire". In Japan, Guam and the USA preparations were being made for a possible emergency that would undoubtedly affect South Korea. Moon has emphasised that no one was allowed to start a military conflict in which South Korea was involved without his consent (clearly implied was: not even the USA). China announced that it would join the UN's renewed sanctions against North Korea. In addition to coal, food such as seafood was also affected.

Kim Jong-un's response to the sanctions came in September. It was the announcement that he had tested a **hydrogen bomb** as well as the launch of a **rocket** from Pyongyang, which flew over the Japanese island of Hokkaido and then landed in the Pacific. But because South Korea had also fired a missile into the Pacific for training purposes, Japan refrained from intercepting the projectile from North Korea. However, the population was called upon to leave their homes and go to safe rooms.

The **2018 Olympic Winter Games** in Pyeongchang, South Korea, offered a **chance for a better understanding** within the hardened fronts. First of all, Kim Jong-un said in his New Year's speech that he was "open for dialogue" and would be willing to send a team from his country to the South for the Winter Games. **Kim Jong-un's sister, Kim Yo-jong**, played a decisive role in the willingness of both sides to engage in dialogue with the aim of joint participation. She attended a Swiss school with her brother and has always been very close to him. After several years working for his propaganda department, she was appointed to the Politburo in 2017.

During the opening of the Olympic Games in February 2018, Kim Yo-jong sat next to Moon in his presidential cabin. Both were watching the South and North Korean ice hockey players moving into the stadium **together as one team**, under the **same flag**, with Korea united on a white background. North Korean cheerleaders then danced before the eyes of the world. A day later, North Korean officials appeared in the president's Blue House and sent a handwritten message from Kim Jong-un inviting him to a meeting in Pyongyang.

The ice seemed broken. In March, Moon government officials accepted an invitation to Pyongyang for dinner with Kim Jong-un. The latter signaled his agreement to a debate on joint Korean denuclearisation, in return for which the US should provide a security guarantee.

In April, Kim Jong-un and Moon Jae-in met on the south side of the Panmunjom border crossing (Joint Security Area or Truce Village). For the first time a North Korean ruler entered southern territory. This **third inter-Korean Summit on 27 April 2018** was named the **"Panmunjom Declaration"**. The two agreed to end mutual hostile activities and to work towards the denuclearisation of the peninsula. Also the overdue conclusion of a peace treaty was discussed, so that the formally still existing ceasefire of the Korean War would finally become history. Another topic was the start of joint talks with the two world powers USA and China. It contained the important sentence that **"there will be no more war on the Korean peninsula."**

3. Donald Trump and North Korea

When North Korea announced that its missiles could reach America, Trump twittered the comment that, "This guy couldn't do anything better with his life." He reacted to the further North Korean tests with the threat that he would react with "fire and rage as the world has not yet seen it." He also ordered a **travel stop** to North Korea and advised Americans who were living there to return. This was, among other things, a reaction to the fact that the American student **Otto Warmbier** was accused of theft during a visit to North Korea and sentenced to 15 years' imprisonment but was then in a coma when he was released.

In September, in his (first) speech at the **United Nations General Assembly**, Trump threatened to destroy North Korea completely and said, "The rocket man is on a suicide mission." He has the country put back on the list of supporters of terrorism from which George W. Bush removed it in 2008 in the course of negotiations.

North Korea reacted with mockery to Trump's "fire and anger" statement, which, according to various reports, was not agreed with the responsible authorities as a usage of language. The depiction of Kim Jong-un as a "rocket man" was countered by the fact that the president of the USA was mentally disturbed. He was further accused of being unreasonable and senile. **High military officials** said Trump was getting on the nerves of North Korean soldiers. By the way, only absolute strength would be appropriate in dealing with him, he would not understand anything else.

In his **New Year's speech in 2018**, **Kim Jong-un** clearly pointed out that the USA was within the range of his nuclear weapons and that there was a **nuclear weapon button** on his desk. Trump replied on Twitter that someone should inform Kim that he also has a **nuclear weapon button** on his desk, which is much bigger and more powerful. A month later, Trump announced the "biggest new level of sanctions" against North Korea ever and, if they didn't work, "phase two" would be very, very hard and unpleasant for the world.

In March, Trump and Kim Jong-un agreed to meet after Kim signaled that the tests would be discontinued. In May, Kim threatened to boycott the meeting and Trump responded. Like every North Korean ruler so far, Kim was angry again about the US military exercises in South Korea. Nevertheless, he had the nuclear test site Pung-gye-ri demolished. And Moon intervened to mediate and initiate the **fourth inter-Korean Summit**. It took place on May 26, 2018 on the North Korean side of the border crossing and served effectively to prepare the meeting between Kim and Trump.

At the beginning of June, Kim's envoys handed over an oversized letter to the American president in which Kim expressed his unbroken interest in a meeting. In fact, the **meeting took place on 11 June 2018**. It was agreed that both states would deepen their relationship and establish **lasting peace on the Korean peninsula**. North Korea committed to complete nuclear disarmament. In return, the US has withdrawn parts of its army from South Korea.

After the meeting, critics complained that Kim Jong-un hadn't promised anything that North

Korea hadn't promised before. By the end of 2018, North Korea was certain not to carry out **any more underground nuclear tests**. What else has changed remains unclear.

4. Fifth Inter-Korean Summit

The fifth inter-Korean Summit between **Moon Jae-in and Kim Jong-un took place from 18 to 20 September 2018** in Pyongyang. The topics to be discussed were the disarmament of North Korean long-range missiles and the dismantling of the Nyongbyon nuclear power plant, as well as a comparable concession on the part of the USA in return. In addition, a **peace treaty** was once again under discussion and, in addition, the idea of applying for a joint hosting of the Olympic Games in 2032.

Copyright and legal notice

This work including all its contents is protected by copyright. Reproduction, in whole or in part, as well as storage, processing, duplication and distribution by means of electronic systems, in whole or in part, is forbidden without the written permission of the Author. All translation Rights reserved.

The contents of this book were searched on the basis of recognized sources and examined with utmost care. However, the Author assumes no guarantee regarding the timeliness, accuracy and completeness of the information provided.

Liability claims against the author relating to the damages of any health, material or ideal nature caused by the use or non-use of the information provided for or by the use of incorrect and in-complete information are in principle excluded, so far, removed from the Author. Intentionally or grossly negligent. This book does not replace medical or professional advice and care.